More Bugs? Less Bugs?

by Don L. Curry

Consultant:
Johanna Kaufman,
Math Learning/
Resource Coordinator
of the Dalton School

Capstone Curriculum Publishing
Mankato, Minnesota

= 2 honeybees

I see one buzzing honeybee collecting nectar from a flower.
One more buzzes by, and now there are two.
One honeybee plus one more make two buzzing honeybees.

0 1 2 3 4 5 6 7 8 9 10

I see two buzzing honeybees collecting nectar from a flower.
One more buzzes by, and now there are three.
Two honeybees plus one more make three buzzing honeybees.

honeybees

0 1 2 3 4 5 6 7 8 9 10

I see three buzzing honeybees collecting nectar from a flower.
One more buzzes by, and now there are four.
Three honeybees plus one more make four buzzing honeybees.

= 4

honeybees

= 5

honeybees

I see four buzzing honeybees collecting nectar from a flower.
One more buzzes by, and now there are five.
Four honeybees plus one more make five buzzing honeybees.

0 1 2 3 4 5 6 7 8 9 10

2 + 2 = 4

= 4 ladybugs

I see two little ladybugs climbing on a flower.

Two more climb on, and now there are four.

Two ladybugs plus two more make four little ladybugs.

0 1 2 3 **4** 5 6 7 8 9 10

I see four little ladybugs climbing on a flower.
Two more climb on, and now there are six.
Four ladybugs plus two more make six little ladybugs.

= 6
ladybugs

0 1 2 3 4 5 **6** 7 8 9 10

6 + 2 = 8

I see six little ladybugs climbing on a leaf.

Two more climb on, and now there are eight.

Six ladybugs plus two more make eight little ladybugs.

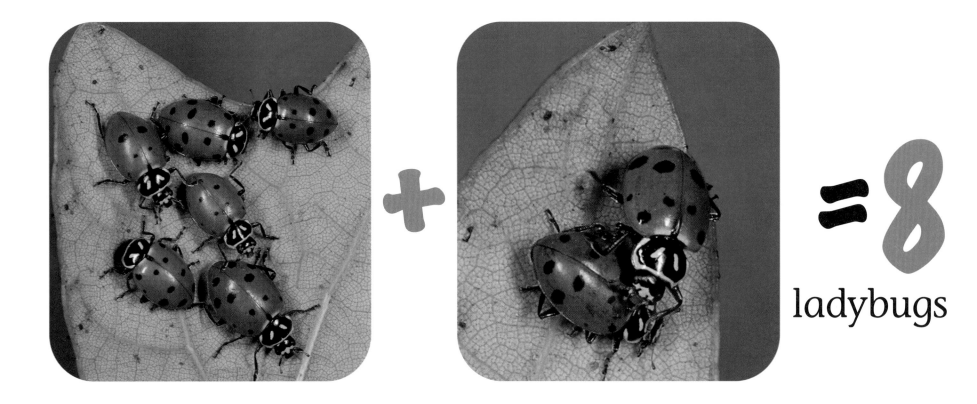

= 8 ladybugs

0 1 2 3 4 5 6 7 **8** 9 10

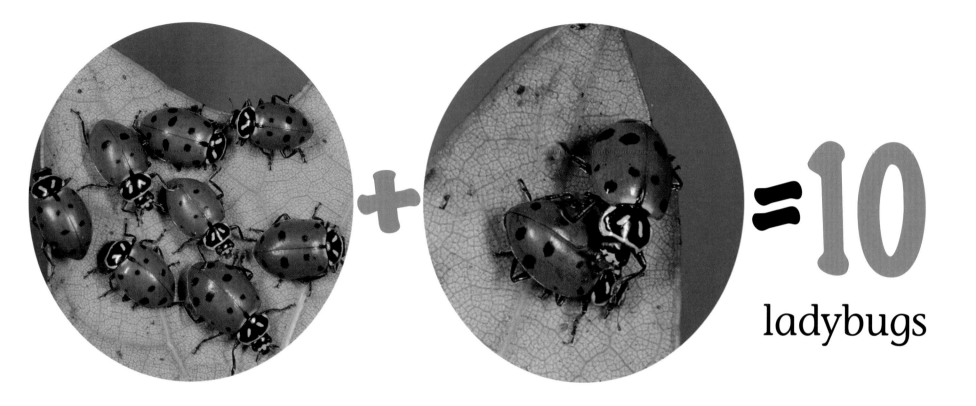

= 10 ladybugs

I see eight little ladybugs climbing on a leaf.
Two more climb on, and now there are ten.
Eight ladybugs plus two more make ten little ladybugs.

0 1 2 3 4 5 6 7 8 9 **10**

= 4

damselflies

I see five busy damselflies sitting on a flower.

One flew away, and now there are four.

Five damselflies take away one leaves four busy damselflies.

0 1 2 3 **4** 5 6 7 8 9 10

I see four busy damselflies sitting on a flower.

One flew away, and now there are three.

Four damselflies take away one leaves three busy damselflies.

= 3

damselflies

0 1 2 **3** 4 5 6 7 8 9 10

I see three busy damselflies sitting on a flower.
One flew away, and now there are two.
Three damselflies take away one leaves two busy damselflies.

= 2 damselflies

0 1 2 3 4 5 6 7 8 9 10

 −  = 1

damselfly

I see two busy damselflies sitting on a flower.

One flew away, and now there is one.

Two damselflies take away one leaves one busy damselfly.

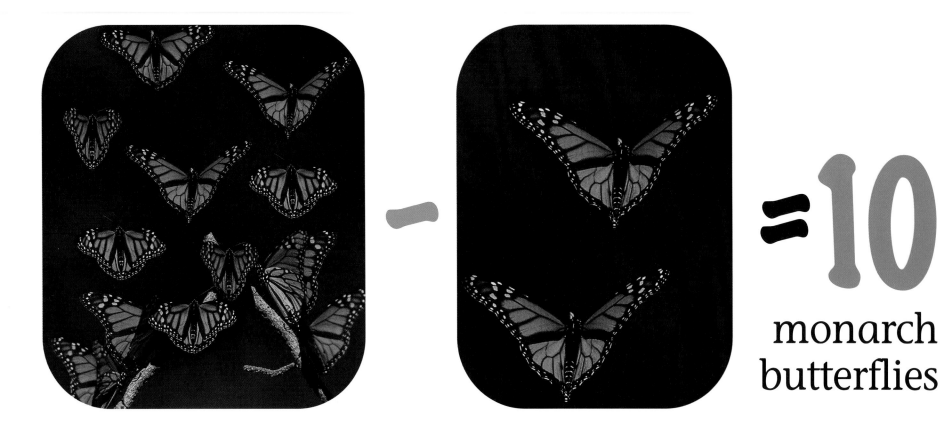

= 10 monarch butterflies

I see twelve fluttering butterflies flapping their wings to fly.

Two flutter away, and now there are ten.

Twelve butterflies take away two leaves ten fluttering butterflies.

I see ten fluttering butterflies flapping their wings to fly.
Two flutter away, and now there are eight.
Ten butterflies take away two leaves eight fluttering butterflies.

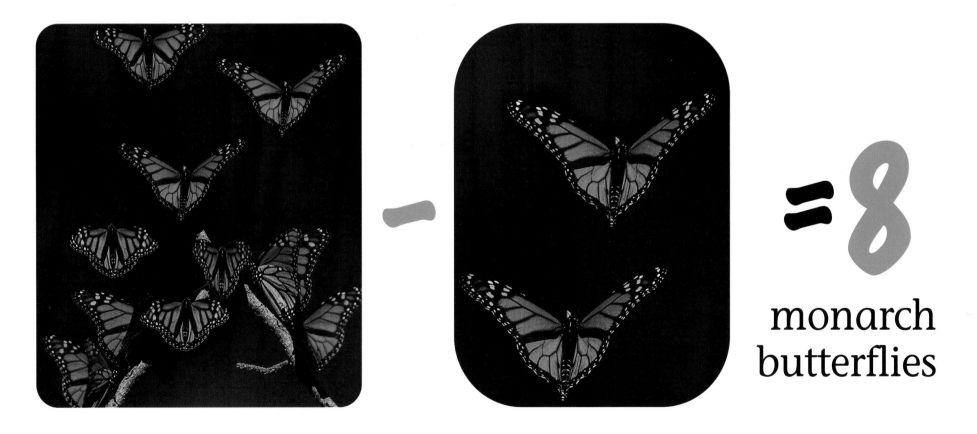

= 8
monarch
butterflies

0 1 2 3 4 5 6 7 **8** 9 10 11 12

8 − 2 = 6

I see eight fluttering butterflies flapping their wings to fly.
Two flutter away, and now there are six.
Eight butterflies take away two leaves six fluttering butterflies.

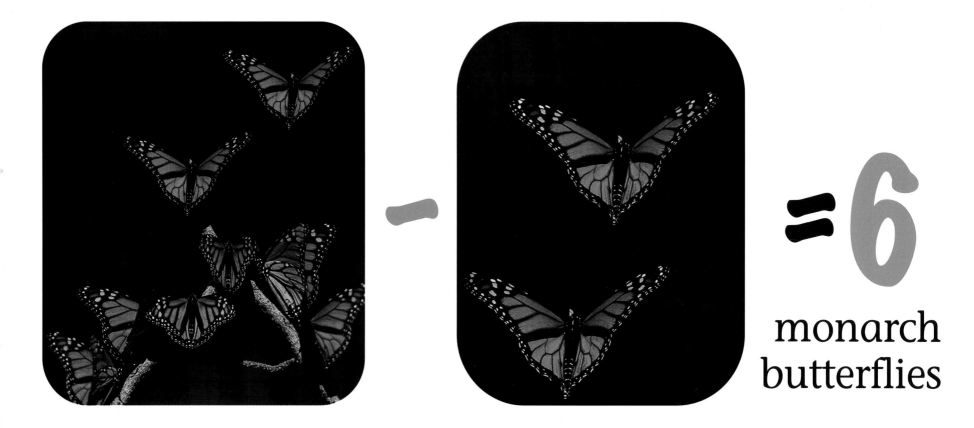

= 6 monarch butterflies

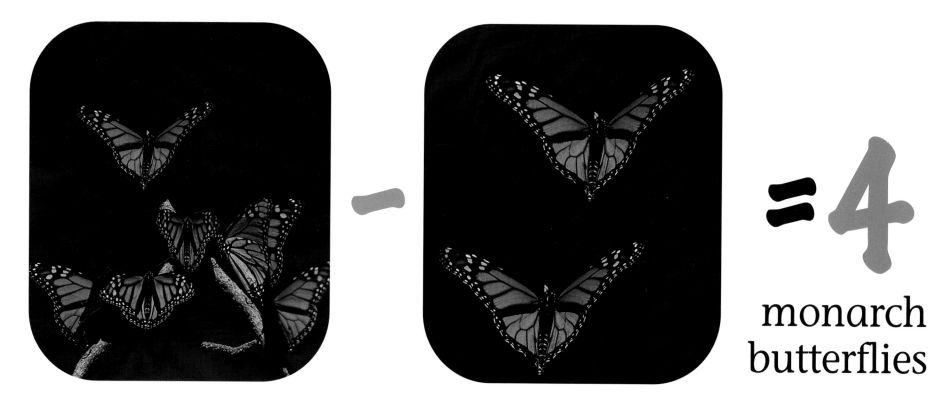

= 4 monarch butterflies

I see six fluttering butterflies flapping their wings to fly.
Two flutter away, and now there are four.
Six butterflies take away two leaves four fluttering butterflies.

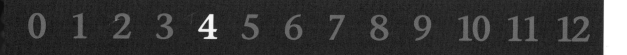

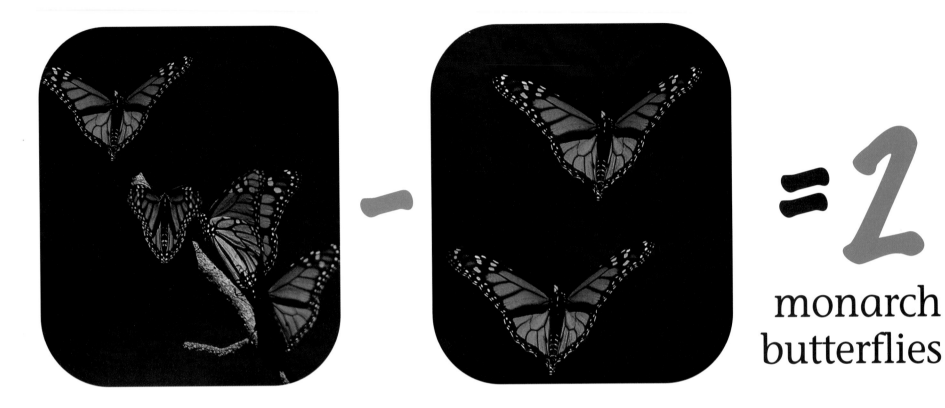

= 2 monarch butterflies

I see four fluttering butterflies flapping their wings to fly.

Two flutter away, and now there are two.

Four butterflies take away two leaves two fluttering butterflies.

0 1 2 3 4 5 6 7 8 9 10 11 12

I see two fluttering butterflies flapping their wings to fly.
Two flutter away, and now there are zero.
Two butterflies take away two leaves zero fluttering butterflies.

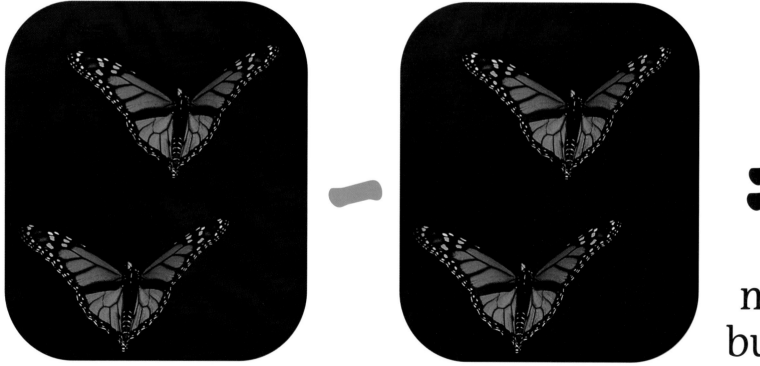 

monarch
butterflies

adding 1

When we add, we get **more** of something. Let's add **one** more treehopper at a time. Count the treehoppers in each photograph.

0 + 0 = **0**

1 + 0 = **1**

1 + 1 = **2**

2 + 1 = **3**

3 + 1 = **4**

4 + 1 = **5**

0 1 2 3 4 5 6 7 8 9 10

Now let's add beetles **two** at a time.
Count the beetles in each photograph.

$$0 + 0 = 0$$

$$2 + 0 = 2$$

$$2 + 2 = 4$$

$$4 + 2 = 6$$

$$6 + 2 = 8$$

$$8 + 2 = 10$$

0   1   2   3   4   5   6   7   8   9   10

When we subtract, we get less of something. Let's subtract planthoppers **one** at a time. Count the planthoppers in each photograph.

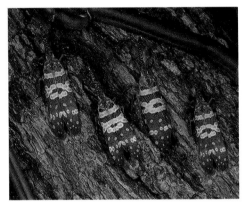

5

5 – 1 = 4

4 – 1 = 3

3 – 1 = 2

2 – 1 = 1

1 – 1 = 0

0 1 2 3 4 5 6 7 8 9 10

Now let's subtract wasps **two** at a time.
Count the wasps in each photograph.

10

10 – 2 = **8**

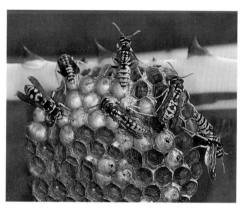

8 – 2 = **6**

6 – 2 = **4**

4 – 2 = **2**

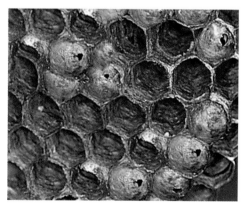

2 – 2 = **0**

0　1　2　3　4　5　6　7　8　9　10

Note To Teachers and Parents

More Bugs? Less Bugs? walks children through the world of bugs while building basic addition and subtraction skills. The combination of full-color photographs and mathematical facts, as well as locational and bug-specific vocabulary, and a glossary filled with bug facts makes this book an excellent cross-curricular teaching tool.

The real-life photographs, new vocabulary, and bug facts encourage lively discussions that build oral language skills and extend science concepts, while developing addition and subtraction skills. In addition, the list of web sites, the bibliography, and hands-on projects bring this book's information to learners of all styles.

Hands-On Projects

Counting Bugs

Materials: • plastic bugs in sets of 10

• index cards with addition and subtraction facts 0 through 10

Invite partners to play an addition or subtraction bug flashcard game. Give one partner 10 plastic bugs. Provide the other child in the pair with a set of index cards with the addition or subtraction facts 0 through 10 (1+0=1, 1+1=2, and so on through 9+1=10 or 10-1=9, 9-1=8, and so on through 1-1=0) printed on one side and the answer to the equation shown by the number of circles on the back of the card. The child with the flashcards randomly holds up a card showing his or her partner the math problem. The second child in the pair then lays out the number of plastic bugs that would be the answer to the equation shown on the flashcard. The child with the flashcards makes sure the number of circles on the back of the flashcard matches the number of bugs the partner has placed on the table. If the amounts are equal, they trade roles and play the game once more.

My Bug Addition and Subtraction Books

Materials: • 11" x 14" sheets of paper

• crayons

• old magazines

Invite children to create their own *My Bug Addition and Subtraction Books.* Set up a 12-page booklet by folding a stack of 11" x 14" sheets of paper in half and stapling them together at the fold. (You might wish to use a heavier stock of paper for the book covers.) Invite children to write the equation 1+0=1 on the outside upper corner of the first page. Have them continue on to the next page with 1+1=2, then 1+2=3, and so on up to 1+9=10.

Remind children that a book has a cover with the title of the book, the name of the author, and the name of the illustrator. Once their books have a cover and equation pages, invite children to use their drawings or photographs from magazines and web sites to illustrate the equation on each page.

Once they finish the addition book, have them create a subtraction version of the book using the same layout but starting with 10-1=9 and ending with 1-1=0. Have *More Bugs? Less Bugs?* on display for children to reference as they work. Place copies of children's books in the classroom library for others to read and enjoy.

Internet Sites

A+ Math

http://www.aplusmath.com/

A Place for Insects

http://insects.org/index.html

Beetles, Beetles, Beetles

http://www.source.at/beetles/

The Dragonfly Web Pages

http://miavx1.muohio.edu/~dragonfly/

Homework Central

http://www.homeworkcentral.com

Insect World

http://www.insect-world.com/

Science for Kids

http://www.ars.usda.gov/is/kids/

Yucky Bug World

http://www.yucky.com/roaches/

Books About Bugs

Berger, Melvin and Gilda. *How Do Flies Walk Upside Down?* New York: Scholastic, 1999.

Cole, Joanna. *The Magic School Bus Inside a Beehive.* New York: Scholastic, 1997.

Delafosse, Claude and Gallimard Jeunesse. *Butterflies* (First Discovery Series) New York: Scholastic, 1999.

Dussling, Jennifer. Eyewitness Readers: *Bugs! Bugs! Bugs!* New York: DK Publishing, 1998.

Ling, Mary. *See How They Grow: Butterflies.* New York: DK Publishing, 1992.

Llewellyn, Claire; Andrea Ricciardi; Christopher Forsey. *The Best Book of Bugs.* New York: Larousse Kingfisher Chambers, 1998.

Preller, James. *What's Bugging You?* New York: Scholastic, 1999.

Robertson, Matthew. *The Big Book of Bugs.* New York: Welcome Enterprises, 1999.

Taylor, Barbara. *Nature Watch: Spiders.* New York: Lorenz Books, 1999.

Glossary

Ladybug

- Ladybugs are beetles that are also called ladybird beetles. There are approximately 5,000 varieties of beetle in the world. Ladybugs belong to the *Coccinellidae* family and to the order *Coleoptera,* which includes all beetles.

- Ladybugs are shaped like a ball cut in half and can grow to be 0.4 in. (10 mm) long. They have short legs and are usually brightly colored with black, yellow, or reddish markings. Ladybugs are generally carnivores (meat eaters) that eat many common garden pests, like aphids, though a few individual species do eat plants.

- Beetles are found in nearly all parts of the world, except in very cold places like Antarctica and on the highest mountain peaks. Many species are found in temperate environments (places with four seasons), but the greatest number of individual species of ladybugs are found in the tropics where it is very warm.

Monarch Butterfly

- Monarch butterflies are members of the *Danaidae* family of milkweed butterflies. Monarchs belong to the order *Lepidoptera,* which includes all butterflies and moths.

- The monarch's wingspan can grow up to 4 in. (10 cm). The reddish-brown wings, marked by black veins and a black border with two rows of spots, warn predators of the insect's bad taste. The monarch has a tongue like a straw called a proboscis that it uses to drink nectar from flowers. The monarch has six legs and two antennae. The monarch has four wings.

- Monarch butterflies are found throughout the world but are mainly found in North, Central, and South America.

Honeybee

- Honeybees belong to the *Apidae* family, which includes all bees that make honey. Honeybees are flying insects that belong to the order *Hymenoptera* and are related to wasps, hornets, and ants.

- Honeybees have short, thick bodies covered with hair and, like all insects, six legs and three body parts: head, thorax, and abdomen. Honeybees have two pair of wings. One pair is attached to each of the last two parts of the thorax, but the front and back wings are joined so that they may look like only one. The fast movements of the wings make a humming sound in flight. Honeybees can fly as fast as 12 mph (20 kph). Honeybees have two large compound eyes (meaning there are several eyes in one) and three simple eyes (meaning there is one single eye), or ocelli, on top of the head. Their front legs and antennae, as well as their proboscises (mouths), are used for tasting. On the lower part of their heads, honeybees have biting jaws (mandibles) and a mouth-tongue (proboscis) which they use for drinking. The thorax has three parts, each with a pair of legs. A tiny waist connects the thorax and abdomen. Honeybees can grow to be 1 in. (2.5 cm) long. Honeybees are dark brown with dark yellow stripes.

- There are more than 20,000 species of bees, and they are found all over the world, except in Antarctica.

Damselfly

- Damselflies belong to the *Calopterygidae*, *Coenagrionidae*, and *Lestidae* families of the order *Odonata* (from the Greek word *odon* meaning *tooth* because of the way in which they kill and eat their prey). The order *Odonata* includes all dragonflies and damselflies.

- Damselflies are insects and have three body parts: a head, a thorax with four wings and six legs, and an abdomen. Damselflies can be as large as 5 in. (12.7 cm) long. Their front and rear wings can be operated separately. When they rest, damselflies hold their wings over their backs, either together or spread out in a V-shape. Damselflies usually stay close to the surface of the water. Damselflies are predators that catch small insects while in flight.

- There are 4,870 known species of *Odonata*. Damselflies are found in all temperate and tropical regions of the world.

Ironclad Beetle

- Ironclad beetles belong to the *Zopheridae* family and the order *Coleoptera,* which includes all beetles. Beetles make up approximately one-fifth of the living things in the world.

- Ironclad beetles can grow to a little more than 1 in. (2.5 cm) long. The body of the ironclad beetle is black with a white spotted pattern that helps it blend in with the bark of the trees among which it lives. The ironclad beetle gets its name from the fact that its exoskeleton (a skeleton that is on the outside of the body) is extremely hard and is its main form of protection from predators.

- Ironclad beetles are found in the southwestern United States, including California, Texas, and Mexico. They feed on the lichen (a kind of fungus) that grows on the trunks of trees and the sides of wooden houses.

Treehopper

- Treehoppers are a diverse group of plant-feeding insects with 3,200 species worldwide. Treehoppers are placed in three families, *Melizoderidae, Aetalionidae,* and *Membracidae*. The *Membracidae* family is the largest and most widespread.

- Most treehopper species can be identified by the shape and color of their pronotum (the area on the top of the head), which often has spines or bulbs. Individual treehoppers usually live for only a few months, but treehoppers have been around for at least 40 million years. Treehoppers lay eggs at least once a year. The eggs are either inserted into a plant or attached to the surface of a plant.

- Treehoppers are found in forest or savanna habitats, particularly in the tropics, where they use a wide variety of tree species as their food and shelter. While treehoppers are mainly tropical insects, some species are found in temperate regions of North and South America, Australia, Africa, and Asia.

Fulgorid Planthopper

- Fulgorid planthoppers belong to the *Derbidae* family. All planthoppers, leafhoppers, cicadas, aphids, and treehoppers belong to the order *Homoptera*.

- Fulgorid planthoppers can grow to be 1.5 in. (4 cm) long. They have a wavy tail that seems to be light-filled (they actually have no light) and large colorful heads. Fulgorid planthoppers rub their wings together to make a sound. Fulgorid planthoppers fly and are most active just after the sun sets. These planthoppers make a powdery wax that comes out of their abdomen. This wax is used to coat their eggs, which are then covered with tree bark and dropped into the crevice of a leaf (often of a banana tree). The nymphs (or the young) use the wax to line the leaf to keep them dry while they suck juices from the plant on which they were laid.

- Fulgorid planthoppers are found throughout the Pacific Islands, including the Hawaiian Islands, Micronesia, Guam, and Samoa. Fulgorid planthoppers are one of 32,000 species of *Homoptera*. *Homoptera* are found wherever plants grow. There are, however, no *Homoptera* that live in water.

Paper Wasp

- Paper wasps belong to the *Vespidae* family (along with all wasps and hornets) and to the order of insects called *Hymenoptera*, which includes bumblebees, honeybees, ants, sawflies, and ichneumon flies. Most members of the *Vespidae* family live in a system where workers serve a queen and form colonies which last for just one summer.

- Paper wasps are insects. The paper wasp is usually about 1 in. (2.5 cm) long. The queens (or egg-laying females) are larger than the workers. Both queens and workers have a poison sac and retractable stinger (they can pull it inside their bodies) at the tip of the abdomen. They can give a painful sting when disturbed. Once a paper wasp has used its stinger, it dies. The paper wasp has long legs and a small waist. The paper wasp has bright yellow and black strips covering most of its body. The black and yellow pattern is a warning sign to predators, such as birds, that the insect is poisonous. The yellow and black stripes are often copied by other insects to scare away predators.

- Paper wasps prefer to live in or near orchards or vineyards. They hang their paper nests under the eaves of buildings, in attics, or under tree branches or vines. Each nest hangs like an open umbrella from a pedicel (a thin stalk or stem) and has open cells that can be seen from beneath the nest. White, legless, grub-like larvae sometimes can be seen from below. The nest rarely gets bigger than the size of an open adult human hand. Populations of paper wasps in a single hive can vary from 15 to 200 wasps. Most species won't bother humans, but they can be a problem when they nest over doorways because sudden movements or bumping into the hive will cause them to defend it.

Index

adding
  by one 2–5, 20
  by two 6–9, 21

beetles 27, 29

damselflies 28
  taking away 10–13

eight
  adding 8–9, 21
  taking away 15–16, 23

five
  adding 5, 20
  taking away 10, 22

four
  adding 4–7, 20–21
  taking away . . 10–11, 17–18, 22–23
fulgorid planthoppers 22, 30

honeybees 27–28
  adding 2–5

ironclad beetles 21, 29

ladybugs 27
  adding 6–9

monarch butterflies 27
  taking away 14–19

one
  adding 2–5, 20
  taking away 10–13, 22

paper wasps 23, 30–31

six
  adding 7–8, 21
  taking away 16–17, 23
subtracting
  by one 10–13, 22
  by two 14–19, 23

ten
  adding 9, 21
  taking away 14–15, 23
three
  adding 3–4, 20
  taking away 11–12, 22
treehoppers 20, 29
twelve
  taking away 14
two
  adding 2–3, 6–9, 20–21
  taking away 12–19, 22–23

zero
  adding 20–21
  taking away 19, 22–23

A+ Books are published by Capstone Press
P.O. Box 669, Mankato, Minnesota 56002
http://www.capstone-press.com

EDITORIAL CREDITS:

Susan Evento, Managing Editor/Product Development; Don L. Curry, Senior Editor; Jannike Hess, Designer; Kimberly Danger and Heidi Schoof, Photo Researchers; Content Consultant: Johanna Kaufman

LIBRARY OF CONGRESS CATALOGING-IN-PUBLICATION DATA:

Curry, Don L.
    More Bugs? Less Bugs?/by Don L. Curry; consultant, Johanna Kaufman.
        p. cm.
    Includes bibliographical references and index.
    Summary: Simple text and photographs present the adding and subtracting of a variety of bugs.
    ISBN 0-7368-7037-7 (Hard)   ISBN 0-7368-7053-9 (Paper)
    1. Addition—Juvenile literature. 2. Subtraction—Juvenile literature.
    3. Insects—Juvenile literature. [1. Addition. 2. Subtraction. 3. Insects.]
    I. Kaufman, Johanna. II. Title.

QA115 .C87 1999
513.2'11—dc21   99-052181

PHOTO CREDITS:

Cover: Robert & Linda Mitchell; *Title Page:* Robert C. Simpson/Uniphoto; *Pages 2–5:* Russell R. Grundke/Unicorn Stock Photos; *Pages 6–7:* Hans Reinhard/Bruce Coleman Inc.; *Pages 8–9:* Robert & Linda Mitchell; *Pages 10–13:* (left photo, clockwise from top) W. Tom Lewis/Photo Network, Leonard Lee Rue/Photri, Jim Merli/Visuals Unlimited, MacDonald Photography/Photo Network: *Pages 10–13:* (right photo) W. Tom Lewis/Photo Network; *Pages 14–19:* Jeffery Rich/Uniphoto; *Page 20:* (all photos) Robert & Linda Mitchell; *Page 21:* (all photos) Robert & Linda Mitchell; *Page 22:* (all photos) Robert & Linda Mitchell; *Page 23:* (all photos) J.C. Carton/Bruce Coleman Inc.